ANIMALS AND **THEIR** ENVIRONMENTS

EDISON BOOTH

NEW YORK

Published in 2017 by The Rosen Publishing Group, Inc.
29 East 21st Street, New York, NY 10010

Editor: Melissa Raé Shofner
Book Design: Michael Flynn
Interior Layout: Reann Nye

Photo Credits: Cover Janette Hil/robertharding/Getty Images; p. 5 Yvonne Pijnenburg-Schonewille/Shutterstock.com; p. 7 Jolanta Wojcicka/Shutterstock.com; p. 9 Rudmer Zwerver/Shutterstock.com; p. 11 (ferret) John E Marriott/All Canada Photos/Getty Images; p. 11 (prairie dogs) Jaren Jai Wicklund/Shutterstock.com; p. 12 Ethan Daniels/Shutterstock.com; p. 13 Susan Harris/Shutterstock.com; p. 15 Anton_Ivanov/Shutterstock.com; p. 16 https://commons.wikimedia.org/wiki/File:Gregor_Mendel_oval.jpg; p. 17 Igor Stramyk/Shutterstock.com; p. 18 https://en.wikipedia.org/wiki/File:Charles_Darwin_seated_crop.jpg; p. 19 hin255/Shutterstock.com; p. 20 Antoni Murcia/Shutterstock.com; p. 21 (both) https://www.usgs.gov/atom/13896, images 11 and 12.

Cataloging-in-Publication Data

Names: Booth, Edison.
Title: Animals and their environments / Edison Booth.
Description: New York : PowerKids Press, 2017. | Series: Spotlight on ecology and life science | Includes index.
Identifiers: ISBN 9781499425567 (pbk.) | ISBN 9781499425581 (library bound) | ISBN 9781499425574 (6 pack)
Subjects: LCSH: Habitat (Ecology)--Juvenile literature. | Animal ecology--Juvenile literature. | Animals--Juvenile literature.
Classification: LCC QH541.14 B668 2017 | DDC 577--dc23

Manufactured in China

CPSIA Compliance Information: Batch #BW17PK For further information contact Rosen Publishing, New York, New York at 1-800-237-9932.

CONTENTS

CHAPTER ONE

LIVING AND NONLIVING THINGS

Special relationships exist between animals and their environments. An environment is all the conditions that surround an animal and affect the way it lives. Environments are made up of living things, such as plants and animals, and nonliving things, such as climate, sunlight, and pollution. The living and nonliving elements of an environment work together to create balance.

Animals' basic needs—food, water, shelter, and air—must be met for them to survive. A species, or group of animals that are all the same, must live in an environment that supports these basic needs. If any of the living or nonliving elements in an environment are changed or removed, the environment may no longer meet the basic needs of a species. The change may throw the environment off balance. Animals may need to **adapt** in order to survive.

Polar bears are dealing with many changes in their Arctic environment. Warmer temperatures are melting the ice they live on and making it harder for them to find food.

CHAPTER TWO

ECOLOGY AND ECOSYSTEMS

Ecology is the scientific study of the relationships between **organisms**, such as animals, and the environments they live in. It's a science that explores every part of an organism's life. Ecologists study how animals interact with each other, with other organisms, and with nonliving things around them. These interactions make up what's called an ecosystem.

Ecologists study ecosystems closely. Sometimes they focus on a particular species to learn more about its relationship with other organisms and the surrounding environment. They may also look at how different species depend on or compete with other species in an environment. Ecologists pay close attention to everything that may affect an organism during its lifetime. This includes an organism's home, food sources, predators, sleep patterns, and more. Ecologists also study how different ecosystems interact with each other.

A coral reef is an example of an ecosystem. Ecologists study how the many different species that live there interact with each other and with the coral reef in order to survive.

CHAPTER THREE

ENERGY ON THE MOVE

There is a constant flow of energy in an ecosystem as one organism eats another to survive. This series of events is called a food chain. Producers are at the bottom of a food chain. Most producers are plants. Plants get their energy from the soil, water, air, and sun in their environment. They contain **nutrients** for other organisms in the ecosystem to eat.

The next levels in a food chain are made up of consumers. These consumers are animals that eat, or consume, producers. Animals that eat only plants are called herbivores. Some consumers eat other consumers. Animals that eat only meat are called carnivores. Omnivores are animals that eat both plants and animals.

The food chain ends with decomposers. Decomposers are organisms that break down the bodies of dead organisms into nutrients that are returned to the soil for use by producers.

Can you identify the producer, consumer, and decomposer here?

CHAPTER FOUR

ANIMAL POPULATIONS

Animals and their environments are closely connected when it comes to population size. A population is a group of organisms that all belong to the same species and live in the same area around the same time. The size of a population is always changing as animals are born and die. Environmental elements such as good weather and few predators may cause a population to grow. However, bad weather or many predators may cause a population to become smaller.

Three main factors limit population growth in an environment. An environment may have **physical** limits such as the amount of rain, wind, or sunlight it receives. Competition for food sources can also limit a population. Finally, **geographic** limits, such as large bodies of water or mountain ranges, may keep populations in one place so they don't have room to grow.

PRAIRIE DOGS

Black-footed ferrets in Montana love to eat prairie dogs. Unfortunately, a bad sickness has been killing the prairie dogs. With fewer sources of food, the ferret population is also growing smaller.

CHAPTER FIVE

SYMBIOSIS

Close relationships often exist between two different species that share an environment. This is called symbiosis. There are three kinds of symbiotic relationships. When a relationship benefits both species, it's called mutualism. Acacia trees provide ants with food and shelter. In return, the ants use their stingers to protect the trees from hungry herbivores.

Spider crabs have a mutualistic relationship with the **algae** in their environment. The crabs give the algae a good place to live while the algae help conceal crabs from predators.

Commensalism is when one of the species in a relationship benefits but the other isn't benefited or harmed. Barnacles can't move on their own, so they stick themselves to large sea creatures, such as whales. The barnacles get a free ride and new sources of food while the whales swim around unaffected.

In a parasitic relationship, one species benefits while the other species is harmed. Ticks are considered **parasites**. They suck blood from host animals, such as zebras. The ticks get a meal, but the zebras only suffer.

CHAPTER SIX

WORKING WITH PLANTS

Animals and plants often depend on each other to fulfill their basic needs. Animals help plants produce new plants by spreading their seeds around. A mouse, for example, may eat a seed and drop it somewhere later in its waste. Some seeds stick to the fur of animals and catch a ride to a new location. Plants also depend on animals, such as bees and hummingbirds, to **pollinate** their flowers.

Animals need plants, too. By eating plants, herbivores get important energy and nutrients. Carnivores also benefit from plants when they consume plant-eating animals. If there weren't any plants to eat, herbivores would likely die out, and there wouldn't be food for the carnivores. Animals also use plants for shelter. Foxes live in hollow trees. Birds build their nests out of twigs and dried grasses.

Black howler monkeys live in trees in the rain forest. They use the trees to move around while they collect fruit to eat. The monkeys help spread seeds by dropping fruit to the ground.

CHAPTER SEVEN

ENVIRONMENTAL VARIATION

Animals receive **genes** from their parents. These genes determine how **offspring** will look and behave. Depending on how this information is passed along from one generation to the next, animals might display different traits, or features. The difference in displayed traits between animals of the same species is called variation.

An animal's environment can also play a role in creating variation within a species. Climate, exercise, diet, accidents, and illnesses can all cause an animal to display a trait that it didn't receive from its parents. For example, an animal that is typically large, such as an elephant, might be underweight if a lack of rain has caused fewer plants to grow in its environment. A bird that has trouble flying because of an accident may become fat if it doesn't get enough exercise.

Gregor Mendel is the "father of modern genetics." He first bred mice to see how their coat color traits were displayed. Mendel was forced to stop this work before he had answers, but he soon began his well-known studies of pea plants.

GREGOR MENDEL

CHAPTER EIGHT

ADAPTING TO SURVIVE

In his 1859 book *On the Origin of Species*, Charles Darwin wrote about how animals can change to better survive in their environment. Scientists have since found more information to support Darwin's ideas. Animals have special adaptations to be able to survive in many different environments. Fish have adapted by **developing** gills so they can breathe underwater. In cold climates, animals such as walruses and polar bears have adapted by developing a layer of stored fat under their skin.

Some environments don't have much food or water for animals to consume. Camels have adapted to life in dry deserts by storing fat in their humps. They can survive for months without eating and for more than a week without drinking water. When a camel does find water, it can drink more than 26 gallons (98.4 L) in just a few minutes.

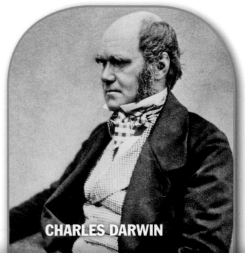

CHARLES DARWIN

Some animals have an adaptation called mimicry. This means they look like other things in their environment. This oakleaf butterfly has wings that look just like leaves.

CHAPTER NINE

DEALING WITH CHANGES

    Changes in an environment can affect animals. If they haven't adapted to deal with changing conditions, members of a species could be unprepared to find food or shelter.

    Grizzly bears have several adaptations for surviving colder months when it's hard to find food. They eat as much as they can during the fall and store fat, which they

1932

1988

Environments can change quickly, but adapting takes time. Animals living in the Boulder Glacier area of Montana have faced great change in just 56 years.

use for energy throughout the winter. Grizzlies also have claws and strong back muscles that help them dig dens for shelter. Some animals, including grizzly bears, have adapted to changing seasons by sleeping through the winter. However, they can wake up if they need to.

Some animals migrate, or travel long distances, when their environment changes. African elephants migrate each year when the dry season begins. Plants don't grow well without rain, which makes it hard for elephants to find food unless they go elsewhere.

CHAPTER TEN

PROTECTING THE PLANET

Humans are animals, too. We have a special relationship with the environment just like other species. People use their environment to meet their basic needs, such as food, water, and shelter. Sometimes, however, humans take too much from the planet and harm the environment. By cutting down trees to build houses and make paper, people take food sources and homes from other animals. People also use chemicals called pesticides to keep bugs off crops. These chemicals can make plants and animals in the environment sick.

Ecologists closely watch animal populations and their environments. They study how humans affect nature and think of ways to lessen our harmful impact. It's important to be aware of how animals, including humans, interact with the environment. All the organisms on Earth are connected. Even the smallest change to the environment can affect us all.

GLOSSARY

adapt (uh-DAPT) To change in order to live better in a certain environment.

algae (AL-jee) Plantlike living things without roots or stems that live in water.

develop (dih-VEH-lup) To build, change, grow or create over time.

gene (JEEN) A tiny part in the center of a cell. Genes tell your cells how your body will look and act.

geographic (jee-oh-GRAA-fik) Having to do with the landscape features of an area.

nutrient (NOO-tree-uhnt) Something taken in by a plant or animal that helps it grow and stay healthy.

offspring (OFF-spring) A new organism produced by parent organisms.

organism (OR-guh-nih-zuhm) An individual living thing.

parasite (PEHR-uh-syt) A living thing that lives in, on, or with another living thing and harms it.

physical (FIH-zuh-kul) Having to do with natural forces.

pollinate (PAH-luh-nayt) To take pollen from one flower, plant, or tree and move it to another.

INDEX

PRIMARY SOURCE LIST

Page 17
Gregor Mendel. Photogravure by Hugo Iltis. Published in *Life of Mendel*, Allen and Unwin, 1932. Now held by the Wellcome Library, London.

Page 18
Charles Darwin. Photograph by Henry Maull and John Fox. ca. 1854. Engraved for *Harper's Magazine*, October 1884.

Page 21
Boulder Glacier Ice Cave comparison in 1932 and 1988. Photographs by Northern Rocky Mountain Science Center (NOROCK). From the U.S. Geological Survey.

WEBSITES

Due to the changing nature of Internet links, PowerKids Press has developed an online list of websites related to the subject of this book. This site is updated regularly. Please use this link to access the list: www.powerkidslinks.com/sels/anim